Kingdom Power Glory

Acknowledgements

With thanks to the editors of *The Interpreter's House*,
The North, *The Rialto*, *Smiths Knoll* and *South*, and to Shoestring
Press, publisher of *Belfast Finds Log*, where some of these poems
first appeared.

Kingdom Power Glory

Nigel Pantling

smith|doorstop

Published 2016 by
smith|doorstop Books
The Poetry Business
Bank Street Arts
32-40 Bank Street
Sheffield S1 2DS
www.poetrybusiness.co.uk

ISBN 978-1-910367-60-5

British Library Cataloguing-in-Publication Data.
A catalogue record for this book is available from the
British Library.

Typeset by Utter
Printed and bound by CPI Group (UK) Ltd, Croydon, CR0 4YY
Cover design: Utter
Author photo: Jean Sprackland

smith|doorstop is a member of Inpress,
www.inpressbooks.co.uk. Distributed by Central Books Ltd.,
99 Wallis Road, London E9 5LN.

The Poetry Business is an Arts Council
National Portfolio Organisation

Contents

Glory

For Jean

KINGDOM

... whose only thought is to protect his country and do good service for his sovereign is the jewel of the kingdom.

– Sun Tzu: The Art of War

Parabola

Galileo defined the parabola as a curve
made of points equidistant from a line
and a focus. He proved that a projectile
falling under gravity followed a parabola.

Tonight's projectile is a metal canister,
fired from the barrel of a self-loading rifle
out of the line that B Troop has formed
on Creggan Street, facing the barricade.

See how the canister arcs, rising to the
level of the roofs of the houses opposite,
then reaching a high point, turns down,
as it finds itself pulled back to earth.

Notice that when the canister breaks
the living room window of the house,
it is at the same height as when launched.
For this parabola, the directrix is the street

and the axis of symmetry is vertical.
The focus of the parabola is, as you see,
the family falling through their front door,
the tear-gas billowing behind them.

Duck Shooting on Clapham Common

That last day before Belfast,
after the dodgems and candy floss,
the coconut shy and hall of mirrors,
beyond the scarlet steam organ
wheezing Waltzing Matilda
we stopped at a rifle range –
six smiling metal ducks
tracking from left to right, then
one by one, diving from sight,
looping under, up and round again.

I paid my shilling, took the air-rifle,
pressed the stock into my shoulder,
aimed off for the bent fore-sight,
controlled my breathing,
eased the trigger
and knocked them down, all six,
toy tin duck by toy tin duck.

I turned to you and winked.
When I looked back, my fallen ducks
had completed their hidden loop,
were upright, smiling, good as new.

Vehicle Patrol

It was an ordinary van, Belfast City Laundry
painted on its side, parked in a side street.
Ordinary, although now you mention it,
heavy on its springs, the door taped shut.

Anyway, there was room to pull in behind
for a smoke-break. They stopped there –
helmets off, rifles resting across their knees –
for ten minutes. Ten minutes, the time

it takes a soldier to crack a few jokes,
finish a cigarette. Also the time
to run a clock down to zero,
to trip a rocker switch, to fire a detonator.

Test

By the time we reach the Ardoyne,
Greenidge has his century
and England are coming out to face
Roberts and Holding at their fastest.

Our orders are to hold the line
by a show of armed force,
to do nothing aggressive,
staying put as long as we can.

There are only eight of us.
The crowd can see that
and they're running,
scooping stones, bricks, bottles.

Back at Old Trafford,
Edrich and Close
ducking what they can
are taking hits to the body.

After the Riot

At last we're on our way back to base,
and we've come via Stranmillis: as we roll
through the gates of the Botanic Gardens,
past the stove wing of the Palm House,
frangipani stains the evening with peaches
and the scarlet spikes of the bromeliads
press against the glass to wave us by.

Headlights are off, gearbox in neutral,
and we're letting gravity take the strain,
pulling us down the long slope to the Lagan.
We coast in the quarter-moon darkness,
soothed by the white noise of the tyres,
glad of the chance to greet old friends.

On we slide, past oak, ash, hornbeam,
the familiar stands of Persimmon,
Tulip Tree, Lebanese Cedar,
until we reach the Ginkgo Biloba:
a native of China and Japan,
a species with no living relative,
unchanged since the Pliocene.

Instructions for Opening Fire
From the 'Yellow Card' issued to every soldier in Northern Ireland

Never use more force than the **minimum** necessary to enable you to carry out your duties.

At a roadblock, **you will NOT fire on a vehicle simply because it refuses to stop.**

Whenever possible a warning should be given before you open fire. A warning should be as loud as possible, preferably by loud-hailer.

If you have to challenge a person who is acting suspiciously you must do so in a firm, distinct, voice saying '**Halt – Hands Up**'.

If the person does not halt at once, you are to challenge again saying '**Halt – Hands up**', and if the person does not halt on your second challenge you are to cock your weapon, apply the safety catch and shout '**Stand still I am ready to fire**'.

You may fire after due warning against a person carrying what you can positively identify as a firearm, but only if you have reason to think he is about to use it for offensive purposes **and** he refuses to halt when called upon to do so, and there is no other way of stopping him.

You may fire after due warning against a person who, though he is not at present attacking has in your sight killed or seriously injured a member of the security forces or a person it is your duty to protect **and** not halted when called upon to do so and cannot be arrested by any other means.

You may fire without warning when hostile firing is taking place in your area and a warning is impracticable against a person using a firearm against you or those whom it is your duty to protect or against a person carrying what you can positively identify as a firearm if he is clearly about to use it for offensive purposes.

You may fire without warning if there is no other way to protect yourself or those whom it is your duty to protect from the danger of being killed or seriously injured.

Note: 'Firearm' includes a grenade, nail bomb or gelignite type bomb.

Church Parade

Today we have the Chaplain telling us we are doing God's work:
God will excuse our violent acts committed in a Just War.

My soldiers are too distracted by the swirl of skirts in the street
beyond the parade ground to worry if we are, in fact, at war,
or whether God will defend them, in the event of a court martial.

The Chaplain recommends we wear St Paul's belt and breast plate,
and carry Blake's bow and spear (he omits the arrows of desire).

B Troop know little of St Paul or Blake, but in any event prefer
a flak jacket and a self-loading rifle. Tomorrow they fly to Belfast,
and their minds are on the NAAFI and their next of kin.

The Chaplain is losing his audience: he reaches his peroration.
God, he says, will watch over us. He is at our side and on our side.

As my soldiers fall out to earthly pleasures, I ask the Chaplain
by which side of the religious divide God prefers us to be shot.

In the Interrogation Centre

Hearing a sound out of place, I open the door.
A boy in jeans and Wolfe Tone T-shirt
leans bleeding against the cell wall.
He stares at me across four hundred years.

My sergeant, arm still raised,
turns his head. His eyes say
'Mind your own fucking business, Sir.
I know these people better than you.'

The ceiling lights pin three shadows
to the ripples of the concrete floor.
Sweat glitters on our faces.
The only noise, our breathing.

Radio Silence

Hello All Stations, this is Two One. Send sitrep when in position. Out.

Hello Two One, this is Two One Alpha.
In position, all quiet. Over.

Two One, Roger. Out.

Hello Two One, this is Two One Charlie.
In position, all quiet. Over.

Two One, Roger. Out.

Hello Two One, this is Two One Bravo.
In position, all quiet. Over.

Two One, what took you so long? Over.

Two One Bravo, we had to wait for the pub to empty
before we could get into the back of the building. Over.

Charlie, more likely they had a quick one on the way upstairs.

Alpha, I hope you're bringing some booze back for the rest of us,
we're going to need it after this fucking caper.

Bravo, in your fucking dreams, son.

Charlie, at least you're not up to your neck in fucking ditch water.

Alpha, my heart bleeds, I'm up a fucking tree and it's pissing down.

Bravo, fat chance we have of a catch here, any sensible fucking Provo is tucked up in bed.

Charlie, yeah, with your fucking wife.

Alpha, you haven't seen his fucking wife.

Bravo, anybody says that about my fucking wife, they got me to answer to.

Charlie, yeah? You and whose fucking army?

Hello all stations this is Two One. Anything happening? Over.

Two One Alpha, negative. All quiet. Out.

Two One Bravo, no. All quiet. Out.

Two One Charlie, All quiet. Out.

A Busy Time for the Quartermaster

On the way out, from the cache
known to him and only one other,
is an armalite, bought in the USA,
financed by donations, smuggled by sea.
Two volunteers will ferry it in sections,
a third take the ammunition
to the place John Joe will occupy
when he marks his twenty-first birthday
with a head-shot at the sentry in the sangar
by the Mission Hall on Cromac Square.

On the way in, two hand guns.
The first, a useless replica Colt,
was issued to a fifteen year-old to rob
the bookies on the Brompton Parade:
someone else will handle the money.
The other, with the silver hand grips,
is the battalion punishment pistol,
used for the interrogation of a tout.
Any splash-back from the kneecaps
should already have been wiped clean.

Dawn

This time it's *your* door, it's *you*
fumbling half asleep to unlock
before a boot breaks the hinges.
You hear megaphones outside.

You're pasted against the wall
as they push past you, shouting
in a language quite like your own.
One, just the same age as you are,

stops beside you, resting his rifle
in the uniformed crook of his arm.
He holds a photo to your face,
says nothing, climbs the stairs.

Roadblock

Every good roadblock needs a chicane
to slow the cars and let you choose
which to search for bombs or gunmen.
Land Rovers off-set across the carriageways
will do the trick impromptu,
but I remember the sandbag sangars
we built at crossroads in the early days,
before it became too dangerous to be static.
Like we did in Newry, where the General drove by
shortly after we'd used caltrops to stop a joyrider
and said a few encouraging words to my soldiers.

Belfast Finds Log: 24th January 1975

Armalite with 14 rounds, plus a Smith and Wesson
under the floorboards, derelict house, Lower Markets.

Browning pistol (army issue – serial number gone)
behind a loose brick, eight feet up, Newtonards bakery.

Martini Henry, Boer-War vintage, could still be fired
wrapped in canvas waterproofing, drainage ditch, Dunmurray.

M1 Carbine, assorted ammo (none for an M1)
in roof space of outhouse, Ardoyne back-to-back.

1500 miscellaneous cartridges
found by search dog at New Lodge roadblock.

Eight electric timing circuits, minus detonators
in shoe box on wardrobe in the Divis Flats.

Fifty sticks commercial explosive, mostly weeping
in City Centre dustbin, following tip-off.

Sterling SMG and shot gun, berets, arm-bands, flags
behind bar at the Old King James on Shankhill Road.

Two point 22 air pistols with four pipe bombs (primed)
in drain below manhole in Short Strand lock-up.

AK 47 rifle, barrel warm and smelling of cordite
under female baby in pram, on the Falls Road.

Unmanned Vehicles on Great Victoria Street

1) Ford Escort (car)

Despite the name, it requires
no further human agency
to complete its function.
Dark, still, silent, it waits
at the front of the Europa Hotel
unaware of its discourtesy
in blocking the unloading bay,
and empty, save for
a hundredweight in the boot.
The clock on the dashboard
knows nothing of the other clock.

2) Goliath (bomb disposal robot)

In mechanical taxonomy
it has to be related
to the wheelbarrow
and the soap box cart,
but the classification is complicated
by the presence of a motor,
a camera on a manoeuvrable arm
and remote steering controls.
The nomenclature is puzzling:
at three feet high it looks more like
the plucky underdog.

Photograph Album

His daughter has found the album
tucked in the spare room cupboard.
She brings it to him, flipping the pages,
calling him from his reading and music.

She asks him who they are,
these young men holding
boards across their chests
chalked with names and dates.

He explains: officer commanding,
quartermaster, adjutant, volunteer.
'And the dates, Dad?'
That was when he had them interned.

She asks how that makes him feel.
He says that it was his job in those days
to find these men and lock them up.
'Yes, Dad, but how does that make you feel?'

Back in Tesco's

'Will you need help packing, Sir?'
He stares at the girl, at his empty hands,
at the conveyer belt where his groceries
have unloaded themselves in their habitual order –
non-perishables, chilled and frozen,
vegetables, fruit – and at the back
the plums, black as blood.

POWER

Laws are like sausages: it is better not to see them being made.
– Otto von Bismarck

Failing the Interview for MI6

Philby, Burgess and Maclean are old hat by this time;
the world still doesn't know about Anthony Blunt.
I'm in a shadowed room off Carlton Gardens,
sweating and struggling to convince
a man who calls himself John.
I'm failing, and fall silent.

A working life passes.
Then John shivers the curtain,
and the sunlight ricochets round me,
magnolia buds making fists at the casement.
John touches my hand, tells me not to feel nervous.
He suggests we switch roles, that I recruit him as my agent.

Command and Control

Who would have thought that Basingstoke –
Bay-sings-toke for God's sake – would be The Hub
for Command and Control if they drop a bomb on London?

Below Alencon Link, a hundred yards from the station,
skulks a Regional Centre of Government, ready equipped
with desks, phones, bunk-beds, drawing pins, tea-bags.

My Minister has come to check its fitness for purpose,
efficiency and effectiveness. He visits the War Room,
where chairs for important survivors stand easy in sheets.

He nods his approval at the stores of composite rations,
cookers, cups and saucers, and acknowledges the amplitude
of shrink-wrapped blankets, lavatory paper, soap.

He inspects the radios, pressing their pressel switches
to test their pressiness. All seems to be in order.
Then, just as we turn to leave, precisely on my timetable,

he asks the caretaker to find out the cricket score.
By the time I can prise him free, our train is due.
I run ahead, along the tunnel, up the stairs to the platform,

instruct the driver to wait for Her Majesty's Government's representative.
But when at last my puffing Minister appears
it is to see his train pulling steadily away.

Speaking Truth: Arthur

Arthur is old style. Grammar school,
then a scholarship to Corpus to read Greats.
Latin tags drop from him like dandruff.
His principled and liberal erudition
impressed Labour Ministers,
happy to nod along with
fiat justitia, ruat caelum
until they lost their jobs in the next reshuffle.
Harder-nosed Conservatives
with the confidence of Eton and The Guards
want plainer speaking. 'Tell it like it is' they say.
You can see he thought he just had.

In the Rambling Letters Department, 1980

They come to his desk in spectacular sheaves
red yellow and green envelopes intermingled
with commonplace white or brown each will be
slit at the top by his clerical assistant the letter
extracted and clipped into a plain grey folder of
course it is the handwriting gives them away as
letters destined for his department and the ink
he prides himself that no one else in the office
should have to respond to a letter written in red
ink or indeed in any colour other than blue or
black the rainbow harvest as he calls them to his
peers are his domain alone the form of address
is usually innocent enough dear sir some say or
dear home secretary others are personal dear mr
whitelaw or mr rees from those slow to keep up
with events there are some who prefer to whom
it may concern he is not especially interested in
what the letters say complaints of controlling rays
from the wireless or voices emanating from the
ether leave him cold and conspiracies involving
freemasons the pope and the current doctor
who are two a penny and not to be regarded as
significant allegations of bugging telephones
or hidden surveillance on the other hand could
be well founded and are neither admitted nor
denied he does enjoy looking at the postmark
once he instructed an executive officer to plot the
origins of a whole months in tray onto a page torn
from the weetabix wonder atlas of the world his
brother had given him for his geography degree
the clusters around godalming and surbiton
were very interesting he is still puzzled even
now by the absence of any letters from leighton

buzzard he takes pride in the drafting of his response always measured thoughtful elegant he never delegates this responsibility knowing that it is his willingness to deal personally with the most expansive wayward correspondence in a manner in which ministers can be sure that has led him to this important role in the basement of the whitehall building he places crested paper and two carbons into the remington types the secretary of state has asked me to thank you for your letter the contents of which have been noted always ensuring his signature is indecipherable

Kindly Call Me God

He's God, they told her, very high up, incredibly powerful.
You won't meet him: he never leaves the fourth floor,
and communication's always through his Private Secretary.
But he writes with green ink, so if you put something up
and it comes back initialled in green, you'll know he's seen it.

As it happened, Sir Douglas Corridor KCMG was her uncle,
which might have helped at the Foreign Office interview.
Asked to name the foreign statesman she most admired,
her mind had emptied. The chairman broke the silence.
'Bismarck you say? Good answer. Now any questions for us?'

Lunch with Viktor Ivanovich Popov

Driving to the Residence, we laughed
at how it might be, in that way that Minister
and Private Secretary do, out of the office.
'Remember the microphones' we said,
and 'Beware of hidden cameras'.

The Ambassador came to the door to meet us.
He was full of warmth yet, looking back,
shy for a man who had worked for Stalin.
He led us to a silvered table set for three,
spread his arms, drank our health in vodka.

Beluga caviar and blinis, chicken Kiev,
Estonian strawberries, a light Georgian red:
and all the while, Minister and Ambassador
fenced about strikes, Europe and the IRA,
watching their words, conceding nothing.

Gordievsky was the local KGB chief at the time,
before his recall to Moscow for interrogation,
accused of crossing over to spy for us.
I like to imagine him late that autumn afternoon,
analysing the recordings, weighing up his chances.

Speaking Truth: Martha

Martha's a stalwart of the Home Office.
Single, thirty years of service, she's carried
every clause of every Criminal Justice Bill.
Martha may look like your grandmother,
but her logic is a razor, her analysis spiky.
And she is shit-hot with language:
Martha can skewer you with her vocabulary,
gaff you with her grammar. Drafts sent to
Martha rebound, lacerated with red ink.
Ministers know Martha takes no prisoners.
Messages come down from Private Office:
'We need to know what Martha thinks'.

Visitor from Box 500

A Friday afternoon. No three-line whips
calling Ministers to the House to vote.
Ours is safely at his desk, reading
police assessments of the terrorist threat.

The diary has an unexplained gap
between meetings on urban unrest and
departmental plans for the miners' strike.
I wonder aloud what this could mean.

Wife dropping in? Haircut? Cricket on TV?
The Principal Private Secretary's not telling.
I give up, go back to recording the discussion
about action on the women at Greenham.

At three on the dot the outer door opens.
A grey-suited stranger smiles into the room.
He waves to us all as if we all know him,
ushers himself through the Minister's door.

Who was that? I ask. Silence. No eyes meeting mine.
I feel like the man in the Bateman cartoons.
After precisely an hour our visitor emerges.
He's still grey, still smiling. I still don't know who.

Footnote: Box 500 is the colloquial name for MI5.

25th September 1983: 7 Honeywell Road

It's 2.30 on a Sunday afternoon, the second baby's
on the way and he's decorating the spare bedroom.

He's steamed off the old paper, filled imperfections,
sanded, washed and sealed the roughened plaster.

His tools lie ready on the table: paste brush, ruler,
spirit level, pencil, plumb-line, craft knife, scissors.

The walls are twelve feet by eight, with two windows
and a door: eight rolls of wallpaper and five hours work.

The paper will slip and tear, blisters will have to be
smoothed or popped, but nothing he can't deal with.

It'll be worth all his preparation and the hard work:
a new life deserves a freshly decorated nursery.

The phone rings. Thirty eight out of The Maze. One officer
dead and twenty injured. He's needed for an official Inquiry.
He'll be away for months. Belfast won't take no for an answer.

25th September 1983: H Block 7

It's 2.30 on Sunday afternoon, the planning's done,
everyone's in place and the kitchen lorry's on its way.

They've conditioned the guards, drilled the escape team,
plotted the layout of the doors, the lookouts, the CCTV.

Their weapons have been smuggled round: six pistols
plus the chisels, hammers, craft knives, scissors.

Once out of the Block it's eight hundred yards to the wall,
through seven gates in four fences: twelve minutes driving.

There'll be resistance, a grab for an alarm button,
warnings shouted, but nothing they can't deal with.

The risk's worthwhile when you're all serving life,
when there's work to be done on the outside.

Later they call Belfast. Over thirty of us away.
We killed one of them. There'll be a fuss now.
We'll keep low. Tell our families we'll see them soon.

Speaking Truth: Hector

Hector is the Mary Poppins of the Office,
dropping into tricky job after tricky job
whenever political priorities shift.
He has the happy knack of taking away
those awkward little problems,
dealing with them firmly, out of hearing,
then bringing them back to stand politely
and give a good account of themselves.
Whenever he leaves the room,
a collective Ministerial sigh
acknowledges that clever Hector
has prevented another sleepless night.

After the Blast

Number 10 calls at three: by five I'm in Brighton.
It's still dark then, and as I approach the Grand
I pick past bricks, door panels, window frames,
railings from balconies impaled in the tarmac.

Arc lights blaze on the gap in the white façade.
Behind a shimmering mist of dust, the rooms
are open-ended boxes of shattered furniture,
blue lampshades swinging in the breeze.

The Front is rowdy with sirens and generators,
whirr and whine of platforms and ladders,
rattle of chainsaws and clatter of masonry.
Early morning calls ring by empty beds.

The Party waits, like families at a pit-head,
cheering at news of someone alive,
groaning at a body on a stretcher.
Warnings about follow-up bombs go ignored.

Later, in a suit bought unseen from M&S,
my Minister will speak in solidarity with his leader.
For now, he and I are silent in the cloaking dust
wondering how long all this will take to settle.

Briefing for a Speech by the Prime Minister
With thanks to the Coal file in the Margaret Thatcher Foundation archive

The Challenge to the Rule of Law has never been so great as during this dispute.

You might like to know, Prime Minister, that up to last night
seven thousand and forty five miners had been arrested,
along with one hundred and sixty four manual workers

and one hundred and forty five of the unemployed.
You may wish to say that this demonstrates the scale of the challenge
facing the Government's authority from the working class.

You might also wish to learn, Prime Minister,
that fifty three students and academics have been taken into custody,
along with thirty seven housewives.

These last statistics may be of interest to Cabinet colleagues,
but the numbers are possibly not robust enough
to make a telling political point.

The rule of law has prevailed because the courts will not be intimidated.

We understand, Prime Minister, that you will want to say that the courts
are being tough on crime. Unfortunately the data available, if quoted
out of context, might be thought not to support your argument.

For example, in the three thousand four hundred cases heard to date
just fifty five defendants have been sentenced to imprisonment.
This may be fewer than the public would expect.

You should also be aware that courts have acquitted six hundred miners,
and bound over or discharged another thousand.
We are confident, however, that all this is because

the most serious cases have yet to come to trial. Prime Minister,
we do advise that it would be unhelpful to call for tougher sentences.
You will appreciate that sentencing is a matter for the Courts.

It is to the police as servants of the law that the credit must go.

Prime Minister, I have some useful statistics for you here.
Over the last five years your Government has provided
nine thousand extra police officers. That is more than

one new police officer for every miner arrested.
Also, you may wish to say that in the course of this dispute
over one thousand police officers have been injured.

No figures are available, Prime Minister,
for how many miners have been injured

Something Strange in the Home Office
For Michael Moriarty

We first suspected something was up when Mr. Moriarty
was moved sideways to run the Criminal Department,
to be supported by Messrs Lawless and Savage (new recruits)
and A. Crook from the Inspectorate of Probation.

Someone tipped us off: look at the Police Division staff list.
Hello, Hello! Three Constables in there, and a Sergeant,
several Dicks and everyone in the Office called Bobby.
All the Nicks, we discovered, had been posted to Prisons.

The Justice Department next. Sure enough, a Judge, a Jury,
plus twelve Goodmans and a True. This was too much
to be a coincidence. Someone must call the Head of Personnel.
I drew the short straw, and dialled the number for Mr Strange.

Speaking Truth: Gregory

You can never tell what Gregory's thinking
behind that smile like a harmonica.
He's tuned into a Minister's mood
before he's closed the door behind him.
His enthusiasm on the cricket score
(not knowing his bails from his block-hole)
comes as easy as 'Quite right, Minister, that's unacceptable'
as if the responsibility for the cock-up did not lie with him.
Faced with a question of principle, Gregory asks
'Minister, what do you want the answer to be?'
and then works backwards to a justification.
You guess he might go in to politics himself one day.

Typing

I'm having coffee with a former colleague
when she reminds me that the Home Office
used to send its letters to be typed in Carlisle.
Every two days the messengers came and went.

Sometimes Carlisle got it wrong, like the time
my taped dictation was transcribed including
'Wales, that's the country not the large mammal'.
Then your urgent draft could shuttle for a week.

The unions wouldn't allow us typewriters,
but my colleague had a portable in a cupboard.
Secretly, late in the evening, she'd tap out replies
to prisoners' petitions that really shouldn't wait.

She checks her e-mail while I sip my soya latte.
In Whitehall, the tea-lady trolleyed the corridors,
her arrival with home-made Battenburg signalled
by rattling the urn with a tea-spoon on a chain.

GLORY

O the fierce wretchedness that glory brings us!
Who would not wish to be from wealth exempt,
Since riches point to misery and contempt?

– William Shakespeare: Timon of Athens

Oxytocin in the Workplace

In the workplace ... getting from foe to friend can be helped by oxytocin: – David Rock

How cautiously it begins, across a table
in a Caffé Nero or the Washington Hotel.
He measures me up, wondering
how far I can be trusted.
We move from handshake and smile
to a search for common interests,
Arsenal, maybe, or opera.
He keeps me at a distance,
until his hypothalamus,
sparked by talk of Fabregas or Faust,
starts to pump the oxytocin
that dampens the fear response.
His shoulders drop. I pass him my agenda,
he reads it, and nods.

Striking the Deal

She's stepped out for a cigarette
on the chrome and plastic stairwell
looking north to the Barbican.

In the marble and mahogany meeting room
Goldmans are expecting her to call her clients
to see if they will raise their offer, just a little.

She doesn't need to call. When she goes back in
Goldmans will settle. She has read their fear
of asking for too much and losing their fee.

A second cigarette. Beyond the City rise
Highgate and Hampstead, full of investors
she is about to enrich, just a little.

Privatisation

The hours have never been longer. The drafting,
redrafting, arguing with lawyers on verification,
meetings on allocation policy and valuation,
setting the strategy for marketing and design.

But when he's home, say at ten or eleven,
he's free from distraction, free to focus on
resolving the conflict between the Treasury's
demands and what the Stock Market needs.

Free, too, to spread his papers on the dining table,
to work as late as he wants, to leave the clutter
where it is until morning, ready to be revisited
over a first coffee, before he showers and shaves.

He knows what will happen in the next few weeks:
the hints in the Sunday papers of under-pricing,
the stagging, the scaling back of excess demand,
the jump in the share price on the first day of trading,

then a steady climb as institutions build their stakes.
He also knows about the after-market: his name
in the press, the quiet word from a Minister,
the calls from head-hunters, the maximum bonus.

Approving the Duck: A Completely and Utterly True Story of Selling the Water Industry

The Time: *The very late Eighties*

The Place: *A meeting of the Advertisement Approval Committee*

The Players: *Stage left: A Senior Civil Servant and her advisers*

                  Stage right: A Water Industry Chief Executive and his advisers

Civil Servant

Good morning all. If we're ready to begin
with your agreement I'll invite the agency in.

(Enter: A creative from an advertising firm
with posters rolled up underneath his arm)

Creative

I've brought you both a poster ad to see
and once approved, I've ideas for TV.

(He lays a poster out with panache.
It shows a duck floating in a bath
with a cigar smoking in its mouth).

You'll notice that the caption is to be
'Register for shares and get some free'.
I think the smoking duck is rather fun
and should encourage registration.

(There follows a whispered debate
during which the sides stay separate)

Water Industry

Stimulating share demand is good.
My legal team and I approve this ad
We hope the Government will give the nod.

Civil Servant

I'm glad you like the ad and we do too.
I'm afraid there is a legal problem though.
My advisers say the poster goes too far
to influence the public – that lit cigar
quite clearly says that buying shares will mean
you'll get rich quick beyond your wildest dream.

Water Industry

Good God, it's just a plastic bath toy and
our investors will all know where they stand.
Even if the share price drops like a stone
they won't complain that they've been done.

.
Civil Servant

That's not a risk that Minsters can take.
We mustn't let it seem we're on the make.
The duck with a cigar just has to go.
It's tantamount to bribery: we say no.

(Gasps and cries and general dissent as
a chorus of investment bankers enters)

Chorus

Dear Colleagues, this really is not helpful,
disagreements over adverts are no joke.
But we think we see a solution to it all:
why not take away the cigar's smoke?
A duck with a cigar that isn't burning
cannot be a symbol of the rich.
Approve the poster please, and then returning,
allow the creative to complete his pitch.

(Everyone agrees and harmony's restored.
Exeunt chorus to generous applause)

Etiquette

Once, a bowler raised along Cheapside and then replaced
meant a chap was in a hurry, out on urgent City matters,
and much as he would like to stop and chat, he couldn't.

While the bowler raised along Cheapside and held aloft
expressed the wish to walk up to Bank together,
exchanging opinions on the weather and the cricket.

If one noticed one's colleagues passing on Cheapside
the bowler would be tipped, or doffed for one's superior
and kept low while talking, sweatband out of sight.

The bowler has gone, and with it our understanding
of hat etiquette. They had business etiquette then, too:
scratch my back; I'll see you right; here's one for you.

Negotiation Skills Training for Investment Bankers

Mike Hartley-Brewer, whose expertise has saved
millions for oil companies, has been teaching us
to start by establishing the opposition's needs,
to present our opening bid as a win for both sides,
to be sure we thank them for all concessions
before we reject their counter proposal.

We've learnt about Gaps, Gambits and Diversions.
Now we're onto The Flinch, that automatic
shake of the head, the involuntary exhalation,
the sorrowing 'I'm afraid that won't work for us'
which must always be our immediate response,
no matter how attractive the other side's offer.

Mike's training will not just come in handy
when we are negotiating mergers and acquisitions.
We have incidentally improved our tactics for the
next round of bonus discussions, and for dealing with
the Mercedes salesman and the Inland Revenue.
Our wives may also find us rather less malleable.

Board Facilitation

In a moment, we are going to split up
into groups of three or four
and sit at the tables in the corners of the room
to do a SWOT analysis
and to identify strategic alternatives
for meeting your corporate objective
of increasing shareholder value.
Then I will write some options on the white boards.

Later, I shall give you each six sticky red dots
and I want you to stick your sticky red dots
against the strategic options that you think
are most likely to increase shareholder value.
Yes, if you like, you can put all your sticky red dots
against just one strategic option,
but would that be the best way
to diversify risk, do you think?

First, though, we are going to sit in a circle,
and we shall pass this ball around.
When the ball comes to you,
I want you to tell everyone in thirty seconds
who you are and what you want to get out of today.
At the end, we will pass the ball around again,
so you can say what you have learned, and I promise
everyone will have something to take away.

London Metal Exchange: The Board Room

The walls are equatorial hardwood,
hung with life-time achievement awards
and trophies for consistent excellence.
The management team sit like seers,
debating the long-term implications
of the expected incidence of contango,
trends in kerb close-out for copper
and the differing spreads to next December
for nickel, cobalt and molybdenum.

London Metal Exchange: The Trading Ring

Zinc is having
its five minutes,
dealers calling
bids or offers
for twenty five
or fifty tonnes
with settlement
in two days' time
or tomorrow.
On their benches
the dealers lean
further forward,
fingers jabbing
prices, volumes
across the ring.
The clock's counting
the seconds down
the shouting peaks
a bell butts in
the session ends.
Dealers laugh and
settle contracts,
trading turns to
aluminium.

Report of the Remuneration Committee

Advertising is totally unnecessary. Unless you hope to make money.
(Jef Richards)

Following extensive consultation with the group's shareholders
about the remuneration of our chief executive,
his salary was reduced to one point one five million.
Where's your Kleenex when you need it?

The annual bonuses awarded to executives set stretching targets
to drive achievement of business priorities for the financial year.
A moment of Schweppervescence.
The average award was one hundred and forty three per cent.

To enhance shareholder capital and returns
Dove: you are more beautiful than you think
the executives have a Performance Share Plan.
We accept that the level of vesting will attract attention.

Pensions: we contribute thirty per cent of base.
Benefits enable executives by ensuring well-being –
Virgin Atlantic, flying in the face of the ordinary
spousal travel, a driver, club membership, tax advice.

Our performance-driven compensation packages
ensure the group can attract, motivate and retain.
The chief executive's package was twenty nine point eight million.
Hovis – Ho Ho Ho.

A Bank Manager in Georgia

Peter Shaw was held for five months
in a hole underground in Tbilisi,
shackled to a wall, unable to stand,

just a crate to sit on,
a candle for light,
rats for company.

He decided not to be a victim.
He shaved with his candle,
practised squats and sit-ups,

memorised the detail of each day,
made up children's stories,
planned his retirement,

played air guitar and sang.
He joked with his captors
even when they beat him.

I learn this when I tune to Radio 4,
driving clients to Glyndebourne
and worried about the weather.

Head-hunting

I'm sitting at my desk one day, sorting CV's into random order,
when the phone rings and a man's voice says
I'm a head-hunter, can you talk?
I say, that's odd, I'm a head-hunter too.
I know, the voice says, actually I'm a head-hunter's head-hunter.
Oh, I say.
And I'm working for a client who's also a head-hunter
and who wants to recruit an experienced head-hunter.
That's interesting, I say, who is your client?
I can't tell you that, the voice says, it's confidential.
Ah, I say.
So I'm wondering if you might be interested.
That's hard to say, I say, can you tell me why your client
wants to recruit an experienced head-hunter, or is that confidential too?
No, the voice says, that's not confidential,
my client wants to recruit an experienced head-hunter
to replace a head-hunter who has gone to work for a different head-hunter.
I see, I say.
So are you interested?
I'm not sure, I say.
Because if not, I was wondering if you knew any other head-hunters
who might be interested.
Let me see if I've got this clear, I say,
are you, a head-hunter's head-hunter, asking me, a head-hunter,
whether I know an experienced head-hunter
who might be interested in leaving their current head-hunter
to work for your confidential client head-hunter
where they will replace a head-hunter
who has gone to work for a different head-hunter?
Yes, he says.
No, I say.

Dot Com

We're meeting in a café: his offices
are chock-a-block with new recruits.
He's saying that the ways I know have gone.
Everything that can be digital will be digital.

If I don't invest now I'll miss my chance
to ride the boom. He spreads his arms.
He smiles. He invites me in. I look away,
to a framed photograph above the counter.

A man at lunch on a New York beam,
in flat cap, bib and brace, laced boots,
flask and tin box set beside him
and by the box, a hard-boiled egg.

Cigarette in hand, he's staring ahead,
confident of what the lens will capture.
And all the while the egg is rolling,
rolling, rolling, closer to the edge.

Industrial Accident

We're here to tell you that we're sorry for your loss.

What?

For your loss, we're sorry.

What?

For your husband's passing.

For my husband's passing?

Yes we're sorry for your loss.

He hasn't passed.

What?

He hasn't passed. Ships pass, students pass, footballers pass.
My husband's dead.

We're sorry for your loss.

Don't keep telling me you're sorry. I'm sorry.
I'm the one with the dead husband.

Yes, and we're sorry.

You may be sorry now, but when you're home with a glass of
lightly-chilled chardonnay you'll be right as rain, and tomorrow
you'll be back at work, and ready to pass someone else's husband.

We do understand that you will be in shock.

Shock? The only shock I'm interested in
is the shock of your chief executive losing his job.

Ah. He's gone already actually.

What?

*He's resigned. He was responsible for Health and Safety and
the Board said he had to go.*

Did they?

*Yes, we were surprised as well. Apparently the Board felt
one death was one too many.*

I can see why.

*But you can't control everything can you? Accidents happen.
And he was a good bloke. We'll miss him.*

Yes, well, I'm sorry for your loss.

Lost to God and Mammon
In memory of twelve City firms and twelve City churches

St Ewin
St Messel
St Quilter
St Hambro

St Antholin
St Benet Fink
St James Capel
St Laurence Prust
St Strauss Turnbull
St James Duke's Place

St Peter Le Poer
St John Zachary
St Robert Fleming
St Bisgood Bishop
St Wedd Durlacher
St Michael Le Querne
St Laurence Pountney

St Leopold Joseph
St Nicholas Acons
St Martin Pomeroy
St Samuel Montagu
St Charterhouse Japhet
St Christopher le Stocks
St Swithin London Stone

Cutting Back

I used to be in HR in the City
she says, drinking the tea
I've brought out on a tray.
Above us, half skeleton,
the London plane tree
which fills my windows.

But I wasn't ruthless enough
Into the wood-chipper go
armfuls of fresh branches,
leaves warm with sunlight.
We watch the whirring
spew of green and brown.

I could see the human consequences.
She puts down her mug,
straps on her helmet,
picks up the chainsaw,
and boots spiking the trunk
climbs to cut the other half.